WOLVES!
Strange and Wonderful

Laurence Pringle

Illustrated by
Meryl Henderson

ASTRA YOUNG READERS

AN IMPRINT OF ASTRA BOOKS FOR YOUNG READERS
New York

Dedicated to Dr. L. David Mech, known as "Dave" when we were
fellow wildlife ecology classmates and friends at Cornell University,
beginning in 1953. He was smart and curious—a good student despite
working 30 hours a week in a grocery store to put himself through
college. Then he began a distinguished career of wolf research, not
just in the United States, but in Europe and in the far northern Arctic.
To this day he advises others in research of wolves and their prey,
writes about wolves, and is modest about his many accomplishments.
—LP

In grateful and loving memory to Mrs. Marceil Pultorak,
my first art teacher and mentor, and to Bob Craven,
my first agent. They started me on my path.
—MH

The author and illustrator wish to thank the following
for their invaluable help in vetting the manuscript and art resources:
Dr. L. David Mech, senior research scientist, U. S. Geological
Survey and adjunct professor, University of Minnesota, for his careful
review of text and illustrations; Jack Gladstone, enrolled citizen
of the Blackfeet Nation; Aaron Leggett, senior curator, Alaska
History & Indigenous Culture, Anchorage Museum; John Thomassen,
deputy collections Manager at the American Numismatic Society;
the Division of Anthropology at the American Museum of Natural History.

Astra Young Readers
An imprint of Astra Books for Young Readers, a division of Astra Publishing House
Printed in China

ISBN: 978-1-63592-327-8 (hc)
ISBN: 978-1-63592-828-0 (eBook)
Library of Congress Control Number: 2021918568

First edition
10 9 8 7 6 5 4 3 2 1

The text is set in Goudy Old Style.
The illustrations are done in watercolor and pencil.

Just for fun, howl like a wolf. Throw your head back and let out a long, loud wolf howl. *AR-WOOOOOOOOOOOOO!*

You have probably heard a sound like that in movies and television programs. Filmmakers sometimes use it in night scenes. They know that a wolf's howl can send a powerful message—of wildness, of mystery, of danger.

For thousands of years wolves have inspired legends, myths, and scary stories. Sometimes they've sparked feelings of fear. Since the mid-1990s, however, scientists have studied the lives of real wolves, not imaginary creatures. Thanks to their discoveries, people's ideas and feelings about wolves have changed.

Wolves and their ancestors have lived mostly in the northern half of Earth (the Northern Hemisphere) for several million years. They are **canines**, related to such other wild **mammals** as coyotes, jackals, and also to domesticated dogs. Dingoes of Australia, African hunting dogs, and dholes of Asia are also canines.

Most wolves are gray wolves and have one scientific name—*Canis lupus*, but they are not all exactly alike. Those that live in the far north have smaller ears and thicker fur than wolves that live in warmer climates. Some have common names that are based on where they live. For example, in the far north *Canis lupus* is called the **tundra** or Arctic wolf. The Mexican wolf and the Rocky Mountain wolf are also *Canis lupus*.

One North American wolf is different enough from the others, and it has a separate species name, *Canis rufus*, the red wolf. (The Latin word *rufus* means "red" in English.)

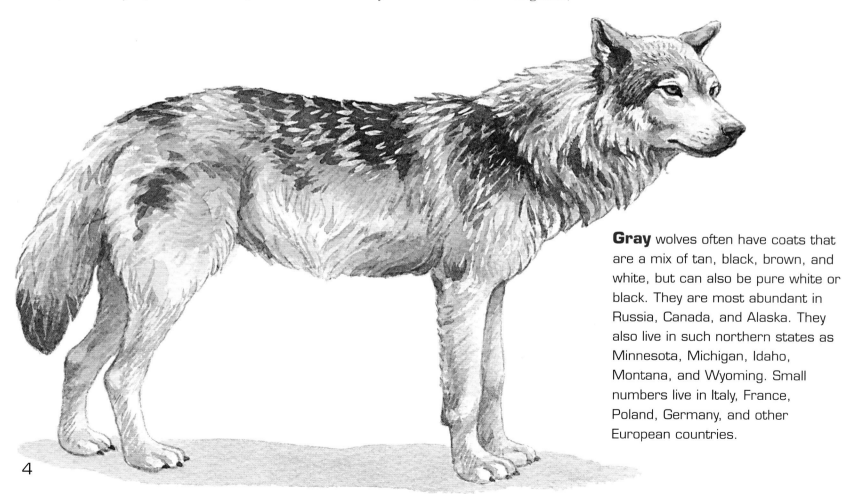

Gray wolves often have coats that are a mix of tan, black, brown, and white, but can also be pure white or black. They are most abundant in Russia, Canada, and Alaska. They also live in such northern states as Minnesota, Michigan, Idaho, Montana, and Wyoming. Small numbers live in Italy, France, Poland, Germany, and other European countries.

4

Red wolves have reddish fur on their sides and legs. Centuries ago, thousands of red wolves lived in what is now the southern United States. Today, about two dozen remain in protected areas of one state—North Carolina.

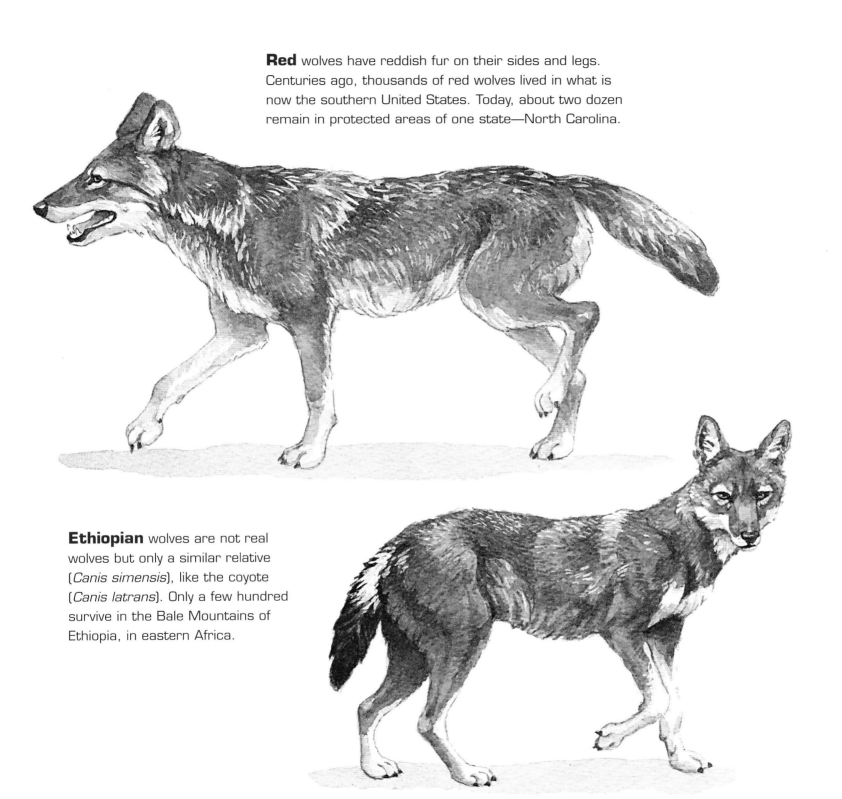

Ethiopian wolves are not real wolves but only a similar relative (*Canis simensis*), like the coyote (*Canis latrans*). Only a few hundred survive in the Bale Mountains of Ethiopia, in eastern Africa.

5

Today, many people admire and appreciate wolves. Some feel thankful because they know that wolves gave humans a great gift: **domesticated** dogs, one of the most popular of all pets on Earth. Wolves are the ancestors of all dogs.

Scientists are still investigating when, where, and how wild wolves gradually changed to become tame dogs. One important source of evidence is **fossil** bones, including skulls of wolves and humans that lived together in Central Asia about 15,000 years ago. This was evidence that humans and wolves were closely linked at that time. Of course, it is likely that people tamed wolves in more than one place on Earth, and perhaps even longer ago.

Exactly how a wild wolf-to-tame-dog process started may never be known, but some wolf experts believe it began when people took young wolf pups from their dens. The pups were fed and treated well. They learned to rely on humans for food, so they did not fear people. They willingly stayed with or near them, and had little or no contact with wild wolves. As the young pups grew to be adults, people probably chose the most tame ones for breeding. This would produce puppies that tended to be friendly with their caregivers. Over many generations, with human help, the transition from wild wolves to pet dogs was underway.

GREAT DANE

MINIATURE SCHNAUZER

CHIHUAHUA

SHETLAND SHEEPDOG

Now, thousands of years later, there is an amazing variety of dogs—from tiny chihuahuas to huge Great Danes. Most do not resemble wolves at all. However, evidence from **genetics** proves that dogs are closely related to their ancestors.

Wolves are **predators**. They kill other animals (their **prey**) for food. Usually they hunt for big mammals—deer, moose, elk, caribou, wild sheep, musk oxen, and mountain goats. Sometimes they eat smaller creatures, including rabbits, hares, beavers, and ducks. And, at times, they eat berries and other fruit. The year-round diet of wolves depends on the kind of **habitat** they live in. In one habitat the main prey might be moose, in another, elk. In Canada, along the coast of British Columbia, live "sea wolves." They have adapted to this rugged, wild habitat at the edge of the Pacific Ocean. They are excellent swimmers, and nearly all their food, including salmon, seals, and even barnacles, comes from salty ocean water.

Wolves are the biggest of all wild canines. They are superb predators, thanks in part to their size, strength, and long, strong legs. When standing, their knees are close together and their front paws turn outward. This helps a wolf on the move, as its rear feet usually land in the same spots where its front feet stepped. This saves energy, especially when a wolf travels through deep snow. Wolves can lope along at a steady pace of five to six miles an hour. In one night, they can travel as far as thirty-five miles.

From nose to tail tip, a wolf can measure as long as six and a half feet. Usually, an adult female weighs about 100 pounds, a male about 125 pounds.

When wolves hunt, they rely on their keen senses of sight, hearing, and smell. They see well, both day and night, and are especially good at spotting prey that is moving. Their ears can detect sounds—like howls of other wolves—several miles away. Wolves turn their ears to aim directly at the source of a sound.

Like all canines, wolves have an extraordinary sense of smell, much more sensitive than that of humans. Your nose has about 5 to 6 million scent receptors. A wolf's nose has about 280 million. A wolf gets vital information when it points its nose into a breeze. It moves its nose from side to side. Its nostrils quiver. From more than two miles away it may catch the scent of a moose, deer, or other prey.

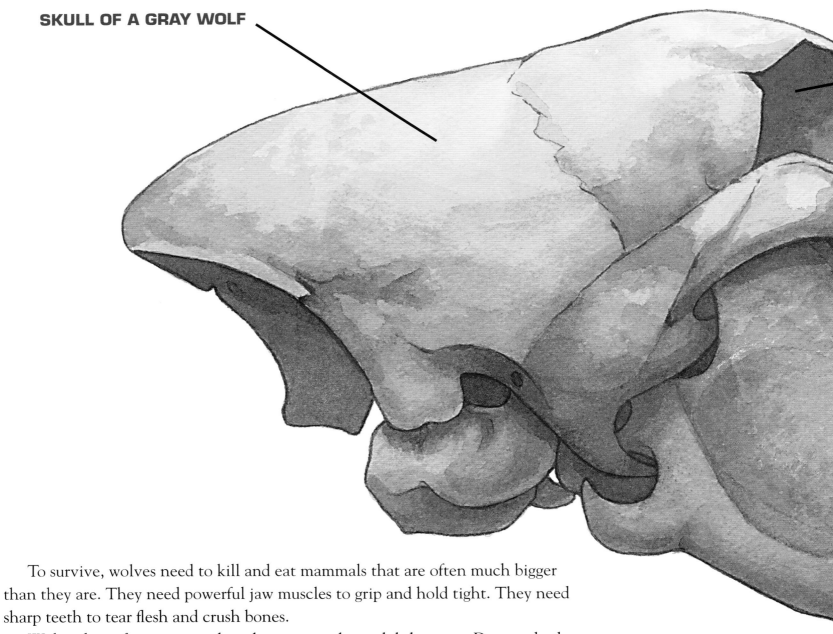

SKULL OF A GRAY WOLF

To survive, wolves need to kill and eat mammals that are often much bigger than they are. They need powerful jaw muscles to grip and hold tight. They need sharp teeth to tear flesh and crush bones.

Wolves have forty-two teeth, a dozen more than adult humans. Dogs and other canines also have forty-two teeth, but wolf jaws and teeth are much bigger and stronger than those of most domesticated dogs.

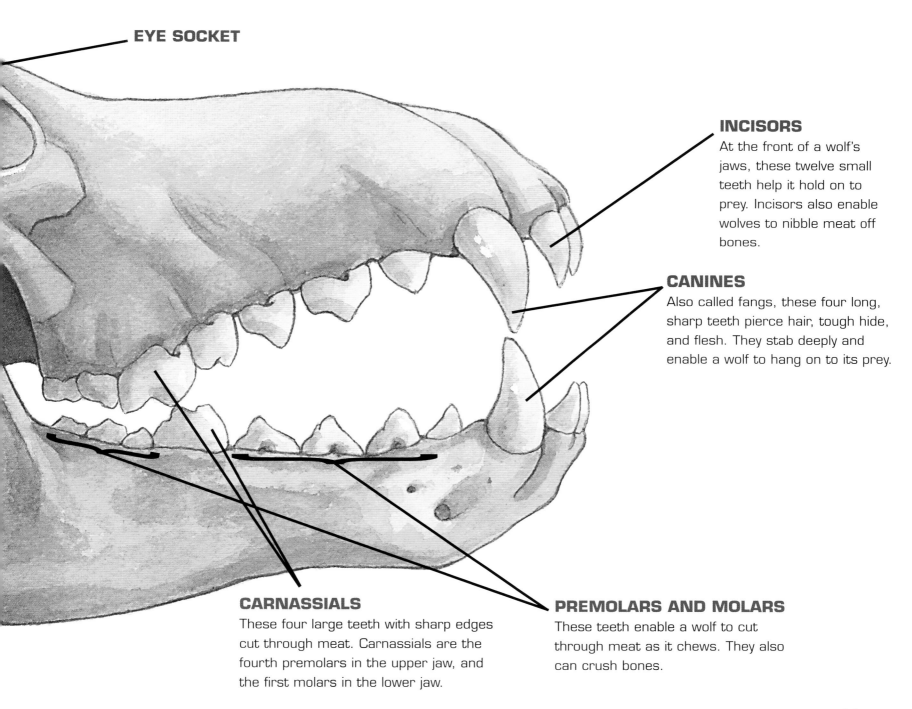

EYE SOCKET

INCISORS
At the front of a wolf's jaws, these twelve small teeth help it hold on to prey. Incisors also enable wolves to nibble meat off bones.

CANINES
Also called fangs, these four long, sharp teeth pierce hair, tough hide, and flesh. They stab deeply and enable a wolf to hang on to its prey.

CARNASSIALS
These four large teeth with sharp edges cut through meat. Carnassials are the fourth premolars in the upper jaw, and the first molars in the lower jaw.

PREMOLARS AND MOLARS
These teeth enable a wolf to cut through meat as it chews. They also can crush bones.

11

Sharp teeth, swift feet, and a super sense of smell help make wolves great hunters. So does teamwork. A whole wolf family, or **pack**, seeks, chases, and attacks prey together.

A wolf pack begins to form when a male and female wolf mate. As pups develop within the female's body, the wolf pair searches for a den. It might be in a rocky cave, a space under tree roots, or one dug by the wolves in sandy soil. A good, safe den is a treasure, and may be used by a wolf family for many years. Far north in the Canadian Arctic, one roomy den has been home to wolf packs off and on for seven hundred years or more.

Once pups are born they nurse milk from their mother. Their father brings food to her, and both parents guard the pups. The mother cares for them while the father leaves to hunt, although eventually the mother hunts for them too. The pups grow quickly. They start to eat solid food when just three weeks old. Returning from a hunt, the mother or father may spit up, or **regurgitate**, some partly digested food for their pups.

The pups play with stones, bones, feathers, or other objects. They chase and wrestle. They stalk and ambush one another—and sometimes mom and dad. They are playing, but also learning skills they will need when they are big enough to join their parents on hunts. This also helps to begin to work out their place in the social life of the family. Some tend to be bold and confident **(dominant)**. Some are inclined to obey and follow others **(submissive)**.

Two parents and their pups are just a beginning of a wolf pack. Some young wolves stay in their pack when new pups are born. For a year or more they are helpful, older siblings. The pack grows. Usually, a pack is made up of less than ten family members, but at times can be many more.

Whatever its size, a wolf pack is a close-knit family that travels, hunts, eats, and rests together. The pack is usually led by the oldest, most experienced family members—usually the mother and father of the younger wolves.

Wolves are very social animals. They rest close together, lick each other's fur, and share food. Pack members have many ways to express their feelings for one another. The positions of a wolf's body, tail, face, and ears have different meanings. (You'll notice that pet dogs have the same wolf "body language.")

A wagging tail is a friendly signal. A wolf wagging both its tail and its rear gives a very strong signal of friendliness.

Tail held high, with or without tail wagging, asserts a wolf's dominance.

Tail held low, or tucked between rear legs, signals "I am not a threat."

A submissive wolf may show how nonthreatening it is by lying on its back, feet raised, belly exposed.

A dominant wolf sometimes has a threatening look, with its lips curled, fangs showing and its ears upright and pointing forward.

A wolf can show respect for its pack leader by closing its mouth, narrowing its eyes to slits, and flattening its ears against its head.

"Want to play?" A wolf gives a "play bow" by lowering the front of its body and keeping its rear raised, with tail wags.

Mother and Father, Not "Alphas"

Alpha, is the first letter of the Greek alphabet, and for many years that name was given to the leader or leaders of a wolf pack. They were called alphas, and people believed that wolves of lower rank often challenged their leadership. An alpha male was often thought to be aggressive.

However, the image of a tough, aggressive alpha wolf came from observations of captive wolves. When wolves that are strangers to one another are joined in a captive group, they have many clashes over leadership. This is not true in a wild wolf pack. Wild packs are not a mix of strangers, but a close family where all members know who is in charge. Scientists who have studied such packs discourage use of the "alpha" label. Yes, the parents are the leaders—as they are in many kinds of families—but their leadership is seldom challenged by other pack members. And pack leaders lead by their behavior, as they protect, nurture, teach, and share.

A long, quavering howl is just one of many wolf sounds. Wolves can squeal, squeak, moan, whine, whimper, yelp, woof, snarl, growl, and bark. All of these sounds can send a message. A low bark can have a different meaning from a loud one. A pup yelps when it is accidentally stepped on. An adult "woofs" to warn other adults and pups of possible danger.

Howling is most common in winter, as mating season nears. The sound may carry for several miles, and up to ten miles in tundra habitat or other wide-open spaces.

Wolf howls differ in tone and volume, and send different messages. Sometimes wolves simply seem to howl for the pleasure of it. One wolf may give a solo howl, saying "here I am" when it is separated from its family. When it rejoins its pack, all of the wolves may celebrate with a chorus. It sounds like a moment of joy, and strengthens family bonds.

Wolf howls can send an important message: "This is our **territory**." A territory is a pack's home range. The size of a territory depends on the number of wolves in a pack and the abundance of prey. Where prey is scarce, a territory can be as vast as hundreds of square miles.

Though wolves sometimes howl to defend their territory, they have other ways to do this. While traveling, especially near the borders of their territory, they leave **scent posts**, which act as No Trespassing signs. The wolves, especially the pack leaders, leave odors on logs, rocks, and other objects. They do this by squirting drops of urine. (This could be called "pee mail.") Like all canines, wolves can learn a lot by smelling scent posts. They take in information such as: What animal left the odor? A wolf, fox, coyote? Male or female? Was the odor left yesterday or a week ago? Once a wolf learns this information, it then usually leaves scent posts of its own.

Territories can grow bigger or smaller, and sometimes one pack invades the territory of another. There may be a bloody battle, with injuries and deaths. Usually the pack with the greatest number of wolves wins, and might gain new territory.

Sometimes a lone wolf enters a territory. Often it is a young wolf that has left its pack, trying to find a mate and create a new pack. Sometimes lone wolves are allowed to join a pack, but as strangers, not family members, they are often chased away.

As a pack rests, one or two wolves may trot away to hunt for a rabbit or other small prey. However, wolves need at least four pounds of food a day, and will eagerly eat more. So, on many days the whole pack sets out to find big prey. In some habitats the likely prey is deer. In others it is elk, bison, caribou, moose, or musk oxen. These mammals are much bigger than a wolf. They can injure or kill a wolf with their powerful hooves and sharp horns or antlers.

By traveling, looking, listening, smelling—and sometimes by chance—the wolves find prey. They stalk quietly to get as close as possible. Whether stalking or attacking, the family leaders are in charge. The younger pack members are still learning how to hunt.

If prey animals run, the pack chases—a chase that sometimes goes on for several miles. Often, one animal or a herd does not flee. It stands its ground. Then the pack leaders rush toward the animal or herd. This is a test. Whether the prey stays put or runs, the wolves watch carefully. The pack's wise leaders know they have little chance of killing a healthy adult moose, elk, or other large prey. The wolves watch for vulnerable animals—the youngest, the oldest, or any individual that seems to be injured or sick. They are the most likely to become a vital meal for the wolf family.

On one winter day in Michigan, a wildlife biologist in a small airplane watched a dramatic scene in the snow below: one moose surrounded by a pack of fifteen wolves. Was the moose doomed? No! After a few minutes, the wolves left. The pack leaders had sensed that the moose was too healthy, too strong, and too dangerous to attack.

This happens a lot in the lives of wolves. Even though they are great hunters, in the span of a day or two, a pack may find big prey animals a dozen different times—but kill just once. Wolves often go without much food for a week or more. If prey animals are unusually scarce, wolves may starve to death.

When a pack does have a successful hunt, this often sparks howls of celebration. The family feasts on the dead moose or other large prey animal. Each wolf may gobble down as many as twenty-two pounds of meat, organs, even hair. Then, with full bellies, the wolf family naps.

Nearby, ravens wait for a chance to pick morsels from bones. In nature, nothing goes to waste.

23

WOLVES AND PEOPLE THROUGH HISTORY

In ancient times, the hunting skills, close family bonds, and intelligence of wolves were admired by people. According to some legends, wolves created humans. In North America, the Blackfeet, Cree, Paiute, Crow, and other native peoples told stories of wolves playing a role in the creation of Earth itself. The Dena'ina people of Alaska respected wolves like brothers, and only killed them when necessary for their survival. In China, the star we now call Sirius (the Dog Star) was called the Celestial Wolf. In North America, some native groups saw what they called the Wolf Trail in the night sky. Today we call this the Milky Way.

Hunters and warriors looked to wolves as role models. A Pawnee song, sung before battle, ended with a wolf howl. Blackfoot hunters also sang a special wolf song, for good luck, before starting out. In Sicily, some parents had shoes made of wolf skin for their young children. These shoes, they believed, would help their children grow up strong and brave.

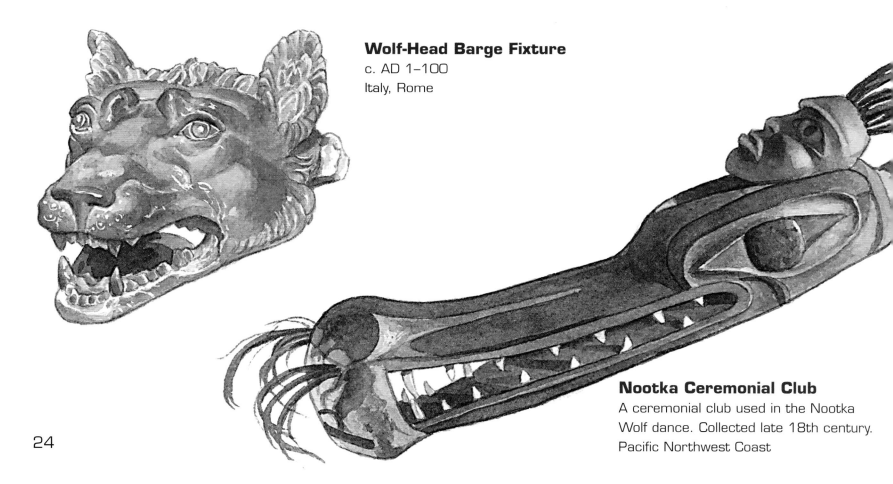

Wolf-Head Barge Fixture
c. AD 1–100
Italy, Rome

Nootka Ceremonial Club
A ceremonial club used in the Nootka Wolf dance. Collected late 18th century. Pacific Northwest Coast

It is doubtful that anyone believes these ancient myths today. However, museums in Europe, Asia, and North America display carved wooden masks, paintings, pipes for smoking, hats, rattles, clubs, daggers, and family coats-of-arms—all with wolf images. They remind us that countless generations of people admired and respected wolves.

Tlingit Wolf Head
Tlingit Visor Mask
Collected 19th-century Gunaaxoo
Kwáan (Dry Bay), Pacific Northwest

Howling Wolf
c. 500–200 BC
Southern Siberia

Human feelings about wolves began to change about 11,000 years ago in Asia, Europe, and elsewhere in the **Old World**. Populations that had long survived by hunting and foraging for food learned to grow such plant crops as wheat and oats. Sheep, cattle, goats, and other animals were domesticated and raised for food and clothing. More and more people lived in villages, towns, and cities. They began to lose touch with nature, and no longer felt part of it.

As populations grew, human hunters killed many deer and other large mammals. Wolves found less of their natural prey, and sometimes killed cattle and sheep. Wherever humans tended their flocks or herds, wolves became the enemy—something to fear and kill. People also made up stories about wolves, including imagined attacks on humans. In children's tales, wolves were not just big, they were "bad." Some even imagined scary half-human, half-wolf creatures called **werewolves**.

These ideas—and livestock—were brought to North America by Europeans when they took over that continent from its native people. As populations grew and forests were cleared for homes and agriculture, wild habitat for wolves disappeared. Farmers and ranchers wanted all wolves gone. The governments of the United States and Canada encouraged the trapping, shooting, and poisoning of wolves, even in national parks. By the 1930s, wolves were nearly wiped out in the lower forty-eight states of the US. At that time, they survived mainly at the top of the world—the Arctic—and in a few other wild parts of the Northern Hemisphere.

Midway through the twentieth century, public attitudes toward wolves began to change. From the science of **ecology**, people learned how nature is made up of communities of animals and plants. And in those communities, predators often play key roles. A lack of predators can have negative effects on both animal and plant life. In the Highlands of Scotland, for example, no wolves have lived there for 250 years, and deer have stripped much of the land bare. Today many places in the US have no wolves and few other big predators. The result is overabundant deer that harm forests by eating young trees and seedlings.

In the 1960s and 1970s the United States Congress established laws aimed to prevent the **extinction** of species, including *Canis lupus*. Protected from hunting and trapping, wolf numbers grew. So did their range. Minnesota wolves spread into Wisconsin and Michigan.

Do Wolves Attack People?"

Scientists and historians have investigated whether wolves attack people. They found little evidence that *wild, healthy* wolves attack people in North America very often. Those words—*wild* and *healthy*—matter. In Canada and Alaska there have been a few attacks on people by wolves that had lost their fear of humans. They had been fed by tourists near campgrounds or scavenged food from dumps or towns. Also, wolves infected with a disease called **rabies** sometimes attack people. Not just wolves, but dogs, raccoons, foxes, and other mammals can become aggressive toward people when they are dying of rabies.

One challenge in investigating reports of wolf attacks is telling facts from old myths. Some stories about wolves from Europe and Asia are many centuries old. In those times rabies was much more common. This fact alone could explain tales that wolves had attacked people.

As people appreciated wolves more, they urged that wolves be brought back to wild places where they had once lived. One such place was Yellowstone National Park, and national forests near it in Idaho. The last wolves in Yellowstone were killed in 1926. Without these predators the park's elk population nearly doubled. Although nearby ranchers opposed release of wolves, public opinion was strongly pro-wolf.

In 1995 and 1996 thirty-one Canadian wolves were released in the northern part of Yellowstone. They have thrived since and formed as many as thirteen packs. Wolves helped reduce the park's elk population and also had other effects. Fear of wolves seemed to cause a change in elk behavior. To avoid surprise attacks, elk reduced feeding on plants that grow near streams in some areas. This allowed willows and other streamside plants to flourish, a welcome change for wildlife.

Reports of these effects, and more, led to claims of many positive changes—*all* caused by wolves in Yellowstone. However, scientists challenged some of the claims. They pointed out that other factors are affecting nature in Yellowstone. For example, climate change has added twenty-seven days to the growing season for plants. This alone could cause certain plants to thrive. Scientists continue to study animal and plant life of Yellowstone National Park, to better understand the effects of wolves there.

Meanwhile, wolves have had one effect that can be measured: a big increase in park visitors. The Lamar Valley in northern Yellowstone National Park is by far the best place on Earth to see a wild wolf.

29

Gray wolf numbers have increased and they have expanded their range. In 2020 the US Fish and Wildlife Service removed them from the endangered species list. This change left it to individual states to decide whether to protect wolves. In some states, farmers and ranchers want to be free to legally kill wolves because they suffer losses caused by wolves. This is a challenging problem in Minnesota, Idaho, and many US states, as well as in Croatia, Italy, France, and other European nations.

Some ranchers have had success using big breeds of dogs (for example, Kangals and Great Pyrenees) to defend livestock. Several ways of scaring wolves away from herds and flocks are being tried. Some states have programs that pay a farmer or rancher for their losses, as does a conservation group called Defenders of Wildlife.

Many people are working to find ways to both protect livestock *and* allow wolves to thrive. And they continue to protect the wild habitats of wolves.

Glossary

alpha—A term formerly given to the leaders of a wolf pack. Since "**alpha**" is often used to describe an aggressive, bossy person, scientists who study wolves prefer to simply say that the pack leaders are usually the father and mother wolf.

canines—About thirty-six living species of doglike mammals that include wolves, coyotes, and jackals in a group called Canidae. The word *canine* is also given to the four sharp, long teeth—also called fangs—in the jaws of some mammals.

domesticated—Tamed. An animal whose ancestors were once wild but that has been genetically selected to be tame for use by humans. Dogs were the very first domesticated animal. Others include sheep, cats, cows, pigs, horses, and chickens.

dominant—Having power or control. For example, parent wolves exhibit power over their pups.

ecology—The study of the relationships between living things and their environment.

extinction—The end of a proccess in which every individual in an animal or plant species dies, and the species no longer exists.

fossil—Bones, skeletons, footprints, and other traces of once-living animals and plants, preserved in rocks that formed long ago.

genetics—The study of the heredity of living things, or how the characteristics of one generation are passed to generations that follow.

habitat—The place or environment where an organism normally exists. Wolves can live in a variety of habitats, including deserts, mountains, and prairies.

mammals—Warm-blooded animals that give birth to live young and whose mothers produce milk for their first food. Most mammals also have fur.

Old World—Europe, Asia, and Africa, which were once thought to be the only land on Earth. Eventually, explorers discovered the New World: North, Central, and South America.

pack—A family group of wolves that have strong bonds to one another. As a pack, the wolves hunt prey, share food, and defend a territory against neighboring packs.

predators—Animals that kill and eat other animals.

prey—Animals that are eaten by predators.

rabies—A deadly disease caused by a virus in the saliva of an infected mammal. It is usually spread by biting. A vaccine developed in 1885 can protect dogs and other mammals from rabies.

regurgitate—To spit up food that was swallowed and partly digested.

scent posts—Stones, logs, or other objects on which wolves (and other canines, including dogs), sprinkle urine, sometimes to mark the border of a territory.

submissive—Yielding to the power or control of another, as pups and their older siblings do to their parents.

territory—An area where an animal or group of animals lives and defends against intrusion by others of its own species.

tundra—An Arctic habitat of low-growing plants, including mosses, lichens, grasses, sedges, and dwarf shrubs. Tundra has a climate of long winters of extreme cold and no sunlight, and short summers when the sun never sets.

werewolves—First mentioned in European folklore, mythical people who can turn into the form of a wolf at night, then turn back to being a human in daytime.

To Learn More

Books

George, Jean Craighead. *The Wolves Are Back.* New York: Dutton, 2008.

Johnson, Sylvia A. and Alice Aamodt. *Wolf Pack: Tracking Wolves in the Wild.* Minneapolis, MN: Lerner, 1985.

Markle, Sandra. *Growing Up Wild: Wolves.* New York: Atheneum, 2001.

Milton, Joyce. *Wild, Wild Wolves.* New York: Random House, 1992.

Pringle, Laurence. *Wolfman: Exploring the World of Wolves.* New York: Scribner's, 1983.

Riggs, Kate. *Wolves.* Manakato, MN: Creative Education, 2011.

Simon, Seymour. *Wolves.* New York: Collins, 2009.

Swinburne, Stephen. *Once Upon a Wolf: How Wildlife Biologists Fought to Bring Back the Gray Wolf.* Boston: Houghton Mifflin, 1999.

Websites*

Defenders of Wildlife; defenders.org

Pacific Wolf Coalition; pacificwolves.org

International Wolf Center; wolf.org

Wolf Conservation Center; nywolf.org

*active at time of publication

Sources

Grambo, Rebecca. *Wolf: Legend, Enemy, Icon.* Buffalo, NY: Firefly Books, 2005.

McGrath, Susan. "Sea Wolves." *National Geographic*, October 2015, pages 127–137.

Mech, L. David. "Alpha Status, Dominance, and Division of Labor in Wolf Packs." *Canadian Journal of Zoology 77* (1999), pages 1196–1203.

———. *The Arctic Wolf: Living with the Pack.* Stillwater, MN: Voyageur Press, 1988.

———. "Is Science in Danger of Sanctifying the Wolf?" *Biological Conservation*, Vol. 150, 2012, pages 143–149.

———. "Meet the Wolf." *Defenders*, Nov.–Dec., 1991, pages 28–32.

Mech, L. David and Luigi Boitani, eds. *Wolves: Behavior, Ecology, and Conservation.* Chicago: University of Chicago Press, 2003.

Mech, L. David, Douglas Smith and Daniel MacNulty. *Wolves on the Hunt: The Behavior of Wolves Hunting Wild Prey.* Chicago: University of Chicago Press, 2015.

Morell, Virginia. "Lessons from The Wild Lab." *Science*, March 20, 2015, pages 1302–1307.

———. "Wolves of Ethiopia" *National Geographic*, March, 2006, pages 124–135.

Peterson, Brenda. *Wolf Nation: The Life, Death, and Return of Wild American Wolves.* New York: Da Capo Press, 2017.

Savage, Candace, *The World of the Wolf.* San Francisco, CA: Sierra Club Books, 1996.

Index